TURN PENCE INTO POUNDS

An Easy Step-By-Step Guide To Create Your Own Home Based Business!

By Phoenix Publications

We have made every effort to ensure that the information contained in this Manual reflects the law of 2012.

This Manual is to be used for guidance & education purposes only and is not intended to replace your own independent legal advice. Phoenix Publications cannot and will not be held responsible for any loss or liability perceived to have arisen from the use of this information.

Turn Pence Into Pounds

Published by, Fenna & Co Ltd, On behalf of Phoenix Publications.

Turn Pence Into Pounds ISBN: 978-0-9571296-1-0

© Copyright 2012, Phoenix Publications. All rights worldwide.

No part of this Manual may be reproduced or stored in a retrieval system or otherwise or by any other means whatsoever, without the prior written permission of Phoenix Publications in accordance with the Copyright Act 1956.

Copyright Disclaimer Notice

Copyright ownership of content

The copyright of this manual (including without limitation all text & artwork contained herein) is owned by us "Phoenix Publications" References to the names of the manuals at the back of this book are copyrighted by their respective owners, but of which we hold reproduction and re-sell rights to.

The preface

List of Contents.

1. Introduction

2. Selecting Your Product

3. Manufacturing Your Ornaments

4. Finishing Your Ornaments

5. Selling Your Items

6. Expanding Your Business

7. Summary

8. Action Plan

9. Keep Smiling

Preface

This manual is your step-by-step guide to a very lucrative home based business. If you can follow the detailed instructions and suggestions in this manual **you can make real profits.** The manual has been carefully prepared and is based upon the author's own experience in this area.

You will be manufacturing, finishing and selling cement garden ornaments. You can make these for pence and sell them for pounds – so the profits really can be substantial.

The following pages will tell you:
- How to select your product range.
- How to manufacture and finish the ornaments to give a truly professional look.
- How and where to sell the items for maximum profits.
- How to expand your business.

Read the manual carefully, read it again and then **TAKE ACTION.** If you do, **you too can make money** in this very profitable business!

Now, read on...

1) **Introduction**

Garden ornaments are made with cement using moulds made of either latex rubber or sometimes fiberglass. These moulds can be used over and over again. I'm sure you may have seen many of the old favorites – the garden gnomes – but there is a very wide range of other moulds available from a number of manufacturers. This can all be very confusing for a beginner - **but don't worry.** We will tell you which moulds to buy and where to get them.

Cement ornaments are very durable and will last for years if cared for properly. They are cheap and easy to make and can be finished in a number of different ways. Your ornaments will be hand finished so each will be **unique**. You will find it easy to sell such quality items, particularly with the advice this manual will give you. Every householder is a potential customer and they don't even need a garden (as I'll explain later).

So let's get on with the manual. Read on to find out how you can get involved, in this very lucrative business…

SECTION 1
SELECTING YOUR PRODUCT

Which Products Sell Best…

Where to Obtain Your Materials…

2) <u>Selecting your product</u>

As I have already mentioned, there is a wide range of moulds available from which to choose. I have listed below the names and addresses of three main suppliers. These companies should be able to provide you with all the different moulds you may require.

1) **EUROPACRAFTS**
   14, ACORN INDUSTRIAL ESTATE,
   BONTOFT AVENUE, HULL,
   HU5 4HF. UNITED KINGDOM
   BY PHONE: 01482 491 447
   ONLINE: www.EUROPACRAFTS.com
   EMAIL: sales@EUROPCRAFTS.com

2) **STREAMLINE SALES**
   101, SEDLESCOMBE ROAD NORTH,
   ST.LEONARD'S ON SEA, EAST SUSSEX,
   TN37 7EJ. UNITED KINGDOM
   BY PHONE: 01424 442 485
   ONLINE: www.STREAMLINE101.co.uk
   EMAIL: STREAMLINE101@hotmail.com

3) **ARTCRAFT**
   POOL ROAD, OTLEY,
   WEST YORKSHIRE,
   LS21 1DY. UNITED KINGDOM
   BY PHONE: 01943 462195
   ONLINE: www.ARTCRAFT.co.uk
   EMAIL: info@ARTCRAFT.co.uk

I recommend that you contact each of these suppliers and request a copy of their latest catalogue. Browse through these at your leisure and if possible, pay a visit to the suppliers and see the moulds for yourself.

The following are typical of the selection available:

ANIMAL MOULDS	ORNAMENTAL MOULDS	GNOMES
Dogs	Plant Holders & Tubs	Pixies
Cats	Bird Baths	Snow White
Farmyard Animals	Statues	Royal Gnomes
Birds	Water Fountains	Fairies
Rabbits	Rocks & Boulders	Comical Gnomes
Squirrels		
Hedgehogs		
Frogs		
Foxes		
Lions		

In time you can experiment with different moulds and make ornaments to suit yourself and your market, but to start let me recommend just four moulds which we have found to be very popular:

Freddie the frog - our best seller by far! A very realistic looking frog perched on a rock (6" high). Very few people can resist the finished sample. Available from Streamline Sales!

Roody the rabbit - a very popular item! A cute little fellow just longing to be stroked! (9" long x 4" high). Available from Streamline Sales!

Billy Bunny - sell these by the dozen! A timid little chap just 4" high. Available from Streamline Sales!

The old boot - a more expensive mould, but easy to finish and very effective when planted with flowers. Available from Europa crafts.

We have experimented with a number of other moulds but have always found that the above are very popular. If you wish to start with just one mould and I recommend that you do - **try the frog!** It really does make a super ornament.

Each of the suppliers listed has email & web order service so ordering is very easy!

Simply fill in the appropriate details on the order form and pay with your Debit/Credit card. The moulds will be dispatched to you quickly & carefully packaged to save damage in the post.

As you gain experience by all means try other moulds and see which you prefer. Whilst we tend to steer clear of garden gnomes (they are loved by many, but are also hated by some!) do give them a try if you wish. There are many people who are making a good and substantial income from just gnomes alone!

Likewise we tend to avoid the larger moulds, as they are more expensive and more difficult to manage, but this could be a good way to expand your business - more on this subject later.

OK! You have selected your moulds and are keen to get started. The next chapter describes in detail the process of manufacturing your first ornament.

SECTION 2

MANUFACTURING THE ITEMS

What You Need…
Let's Get Started…
Solving Problems…

3) **Manufacturing your ornaments**

For the purposes of this section I will concentrate on our most popular item, the garden frog - but the same principles apply to the other moulds.

Let me firstly summarise the process and then take you through it step-by-step:

The mould is turned upside down and placed into a support. A mix of smooth cement is then poured into the mould and tapped to dislodge any air bubbles. The mould is then left for a few hours whilst the cement sets, once set! The mould is lubricated and then peeled off the ornament. The ornament is then again left to fully dry.

It's as simple as that!

Now for the details! Firstly, what materials do you need?

What do you need?
- A mould
- A support for the mould (mould support)
- A tub in which the mould can be placed upside down (mould container)
- A bucket for mixing the cement (mixing bucket)
- Ordinary Portland cement
- Water
- A Trowel or stirrer
- A little washing up liquid
- An old tin can (baked bean cans are idea!)

Most of these are self explanatory, but I will give you more details about some of these items.

Mould Container:

A small bucket or something similar is ideal for the frog mould. Anything that will hold water and is big enough to hold the mould upside down in it is suitable.

Mixing Bucket:

Any old bucket will do, providing it is CLEAN! **THIS IS IMPORTANT!**

Mould Support:

This is also important; I recommend a support cut from plywood or hardboard. Take a piece of board which can be supported by the mould container. Using a fretsaw or jigsaw, cut a hole in the board a little larger than the base of the mould (not including the flange of the mould), approximately the same shape. Do not cut the hole too big or it will not support the mould. When you have finished it should be possible to support the mould by the flange upside down in the piece of board.

Cement:

Most mould manufacturers recommend a mix of sharp sand and cement. We have found that just plain Portland cement (with no added sand) gives excellent results. It gives a very smooth finish and really brings out the details in the moulds. You can purchase ordinary Blue Circle Portland cement in 25kg bags at most DIY stores.

A 25kg bag is about £5.00 at current prices and contains enough cement to make about 20 frogs! You can buy smaller quantities of course, but this is relatively more expensive and I only would recommend this for smaller ornaments. It is important that you store your cement carefully to avoid deterioration. It is quite in order to keep the bag in the garage or garden shed but do make sure that it doesn't become damp or you will find that it will set hard.

Once you step up your rate of production you will find that you can easily get through a large bag of cement in just a few days, so storage then is not really a problem.

Now, on the next page I will describe the procedure in greater detail…

The procedure:

Stage one

1) Wet the inside of the mould with a little water and then drain.

2) Turn the mould upside down and place it in the plywood or hardboard mould support.

3) Place the support over the mould container with the mould hanging in the container.

4) Fill the mould container approximately ¾ full with water. The outside of the mould should now be immersed in water?

5) Measure approximately 3 cans full of cement into your mixing bucket and then slowly add approximately 1 can full of clean cold tap water, mixing them thoroughly together to create a smooth paste (add more cement or water as necessary to form a thick pouring consistency).

6) Spoon or pour the cement into the mould until the mould is about ½ full.

7) Tap the mould support on the top of the mould container to dislodge any air bubbles. Keep tapping for a minute or so.

8) Spoon or pour the remaining cement mixture into the mould until it is full (up to but not onto the flange of the mould)

9) Tap the mould again for a couple more minutes to dislodge any further air bubbles.

Stage two

1) Top up the mould **container** with water if necessary to ensure that the mould is well supported and is not touching the sides or bottom of the container.

2) Leave to set for at least 24 hours (longer in colder weather).

3) When set, remove the mould from the mould container and then remove the mould support.

4) Lubricate the outside of the mould with a little washing up liquid or soap solution and quickly peel off the mould. Do this in one single movement if possible.

5) Leave the ornament to weather outside for a few days and then allow it to dry out completely indoors.

Possible problems

1) The mould sticks when removing - apply a little more soap solution and try to remove in one swift pull.

2) The ornament is distorted - ensure next time that the mould is well supported in the mould container and does not touch the sides or the bottom of the container.

3) The ornament is pitted with holes - cement mix is too thick to coat the mould properly or air bubbles have not been dislodged effectively - try a slightly wetter mix next time and tap a little more vigorously to remove the air bubbles.

4) An ornament breaks upon removing from the mould - cement is not set or too dry - allow longer to set next time or try a slightly wetter mix.

If you follow the procedures carefully you should not have any of the above problems in producing your ornaments and if you unfortunately do experience difficulties then remember your skills will get better with practice. As soon as you have produced one successfully, then the rest will be plain sailing anyway!

Let me comment on the procedure for supporting the mould since this is extremely important. Most mould manufacturers recommend that you support your mould in a box of sand. We have discovered that using the water method to support your mould is far superior since there is less danger of distortion.

I found this out to my own cost with the very first frog that I made several years ago. I used the sand support method and produced a rather squat looking creature with an extremely flat head!

This is was very disappointing and I honestly almost gave up there and then. Thank goodness I didn't! I still have the actual frog in fact as a reminder! He makes a very good wedge to hold open the garden gate, even if he is not very elegant. Perhaps he will be famous one day!

Procedure for other moulds

The Procedure for other moulds is the same except that the method of supporting the mould may be slightly different. The water support method is very good for the frog and the rabbit. For smaller moulds like the bunny, it is not necessary to support it in water as the weight of the cement is not enough to distort the mould. For these smaller moulds the mould support can be made from cardboard etc.

I have adopted a different support method for the boot as my first efforts were not very successful. After trying various methods out, I finally decided on making my mould support out of paper Mache. I gradually built up layer by layer of paper around the outside of my boot mould. Using a traditional technique of wet newspaper coated in a pva glue paste (nothing to expensive here!).

After building up several layers of paper I allowed it to set hard. Removing the mould to leave a paper Mache shell was a little difficult but I found that by carefully cutting the paper Mache (taking care not to cut the latex mould) I could produce two halves of a paper Mache support from which the mould could be extracted. I then built up a few more layers of paper Mache for a little extra strength and support.

This provided a very useful mould support for the boot mould. So now no plywood or water support is needed - I simply place the paper Mache supports around the outside of the latex mould and tie with a piece of string.

I recommend that you try a similar technique with any of your more difficult moulds. You could even create a more professional mould support by adding a layer or two of fiberglass (as used in car repairs).

The support will then last for years. Incidentally, larger moulds come with their own fiberglass jacket supports - but at a price! I recommend that you give these a miss until you become an expert.

Quantities of cement mix required depend, of course, on the size of the mould but if you use the same can for measuring you can keep note of the quantities required for each new mould you buy.

Care of the mould

If you look after the moulds you will find that they will make dozens if not hundreds of ornaments. As soon as you have finished with the mould rinse it out with warm water and remove any clumps of cement. Allow the mould to drain and dry then store it in a clean dry plastic bag in a cool place, but away from the frost.

Warning!

When washing out the moulds and mixing bucket please **do not** pour the dirty water down the drain. A friend of ours who was running a similar business did just that. The cement deposits eventually built up until the drain became completely blocked... a very expensive mistake!

I recommend a corner of the garden to pour away the washings.

So that deals with the manufacture of the ornaments. I have given you a lot of detail so that you can avoid some of the same mistakes that I have made in the past, but you will find the procedure remarkably easy once you have made one or two items.

The next section deals with the all important finishing off of your ornaments. A little care and attention here will pay dividends when you come to sell your pieces.

SECTION 3

FINISHING THE ORNAMENTS

Finish To Perfection…
Scaling Up Production…

4) **Finishing your ornaments**

The secret of successful sales is in the finishing of your ornaments. You will want the best finish possible to attract and please your customers. There are several different finishes you can use and I will cover each of these in turn.

Firstly though, a few words of warning…

There are two potential problems with cement. It is very alkaline (opposite of acid) and also holds a great deal of water. If you choose to paint your ornaments, you must first make sure that it has had at least a few days to weather outdoors as this will reduce the alkalinity.

You also must then let it dry out thoroughly indoors before painting. If you do not follow these instructions you may find that the paint begins to peel off after a few weeks. Your customers, quite rightly, will NOT be satisfied with this; after all would you be!

We have spent a long time investigating this problem. I have spoken to the manufacturers and to the Building Research Council (who are not often called upon to advise on peeling frogs!) I have also subjected six identical ornaments to a stability test in the garden. I took six ornaments all manufactured at the same time and finished them with different combinations of paint and varnish. I coded each so that I would know which was which and then left them outside for 6 months, checking them each month.

All our investigations have led to the conclusion that weathering and drying out as described is vital for a good finish. Even with this process you may find the odd ornament with peeling paint. I always offer to replace an ornament if the customer complains – it's worthwhile in the long run to build a reputation as an honest and reliable business person.

Now to the different finishes……..

Painted finishes

You will find that the painted ornaments sell best since they will be far superior in appearance to many ornaments on sale in garden shops.

The frog can look superb with a black base, green skin and a little black and yellow to bring out the eyes.

A little imagination with the other colours for the different ornaments can transform the rather dull appearance of the cement and turn them into very saleable items.

I prefer to use proper cement paint when possible and I find that International's concrete paint is ideal (available from most DIY shops), but really any brand of concrete paint will suffice.

An example for painting the frog I use black on the base and leaf green for the skin. I then paint the eyes with a little yellow (ordinary household paint) and finally pick out the pupils in black. This really brings the frog to life.

A few tips on painting the frog.

Start with the black base – you needn't worry if the black 'spills' onto the body of the frog. When dry, paint the body green, cutting in carefully around the base. Take a little care with the webbed feet – your patience will be rewarded when you come to sell. Once the green is dry, pick out the eyes in yellow and finally add black pupils. I usually leave the base of the frog unpainted but if for indoor use (more of this later) it's a nice touch to finish the base with a piece of felt cut to shape and glued in place. Finish the ornament with a gloss varnish if you like the 'wet look' – ideal for frogs.

The rabbits are finished in black, grey or white, again with the eyes picked out (pink is a good colour.)

Coloured varnish

We have found that the boot and baby bunny look better if they are finished with a couple of coats of coloured varnish (we use Ronseal's Chestnut varnish.) the varnish allows some of the detail and texture to show through – very effective on these models. A brown paint tends to look too heavy and bland on these ornaments. You can still pick out the eyes of the bunny in a suitable colour – we usually do them in black.

The coloured varnished technique is very quick as a couple of coats should suffice.

Coloured cement

A different effect can be achieved by adding colouring powder to your cement mix before pouring into the mould. With this technique you can produce ornaments in a number of different colours as with modern patio slabs. I prefer painted ornaments but coloured cement is very quick as it needs no further finishing.

Plain cement

Perhaps the easiest finish is the plain greyish-white appearance of the Portland cement with no added colour and no other finishing. This is particularly suitable for larger items such as plant troughs and bird baths.

I don't recommend this for smaller ornaments but it does save time. You may decide to sell some ornaments unfinished at a slightly cheaper price.

Experiment a little with different finishes and see which you and your customers prefer. You may choose to build up a stock of items with different finishes to suit your customers' choice. You can always decide to price your ornaments according to the time spent upon them i.e. painted ornaments at a higher price (more of this later.)

Scaling up production

Before we leave the topic of manufacturing and finishing the ornaments, a word about 'production planning.' You may feel that the process is rather 'long winded.' In a sense you are correct, but your output can be increased significantly as you gain experience and as you purchase more moulds. You should aim to make the items in batches. As soon as you can afford it buy a second mould and then a third and so on. Set up your moulds each in their own support.

Mix up one batch of cement for the whole lot (quantities for 4 or 5 moulds should be quite manageable) and fill the moulds one by one. Tap each to expel air bubbles and leave to set. In this way you can make 5 ornaments in about the same time as it takes to make one. When finishing, again paint in batches where possible. For example, wait until you have 5 frogs ready for painting and then do all the bases together, followed by all the bodies etc.

Since most of the time is taken up in setting, drying and weathering, the workload is not enormous. It should be quite possible in time to make about 5 ornaments a day (25-30 a week in only a few hours work.) In time you will have a series of batches on the go – setting, weathering, drying and painting so that no time is wasted.

Work out a programme to suit yourself – Remember, **you are in control!** With a little practice you will soon find it very simple to manufacture and finish your ornaments and you will soon have a large stock of items to sell. So let's move on to the all important techniques for selling your goods……..

SECTION 4

SELLING THE ITEMS

The Price To Charge…

How & Where To Sell…

5) Selling your items

In many ways this is the most important part of the manual – you must achieve good sales to produce a healthy income. There are a number of ways of selling your ornaments and I will review these one by one.

Selling by word of mouth

We have found this to be very effective, mainly because the ornaments look so good when properly finished. Once you have a small stock – maybe just 3 or 4 items – start showing them to your friends and neighbours. Most will be surprised when you tell them that you make the ornaments yourself – and many will be quite happy to buy from you, either for themselves or as a gift for someone. Every time you sell an item try to persuade your customer to find one more order for you (you might even offer a small commission on each new order.) You should soon find that this process brings in a steady stream of orders – your 'bread and butter' sales.

If you belong to a club or organisation – don't be shy – take a sample along to your next meeting and make a few more sales. The ornaments make unusual gifts for birthdays or Christmas. I recommend that you pass some on as gifts, again encouraging people to obtain more orders for you.

Always ensure that your ornaments are well finished and in good condition and you will find many willing purchasers.

Selling through shops

You should find that one or more local shops would be willing to sell your ornaments for you. The most obvious outlet may be a craft shop for the smaller items, but you should also consider greengrocers, florists, or indeed any local store. It is probably best to concentrate on small family owned businesses rather than large chains.

Make sure that your approach is business-like – book an appointment to see the manager or owner and make sure that your samples are in tip top condition. Work out the terms you require in advance, but be prepared to negotiate the price or commission. Make sure that you know how many items you can supply initially and the rate at which you can produce more when necessary.

- Commission sales (split when sold) – here you supply the shopkeeper with as many items as they wish to keep in stock (at no charge.) they sell the items for you at an agreed price and pass a proportion of the money to you, keeping a commission for themselves.

  The profit margin on these items is so good that you can afford to pay a commission of say 20-25%, but try to negotiate a smaller commission if you can.

- Straight sale – this means that you simply sell to the shopkeeper at an agreed price. The shopkeeper is then free to sell the items at whatever price they wish and to keep the proceeds. You could always agree to buy back any unsold items if you wish.

Selling through Garden Centre's

The same principles apply to selling through Garden Centre's. Visit the local Centre's in your area. Check to see which are already selling ornaments and compare the quality and price. Don't be afraid to approach these shops as **your** ornaments are likely to be superior. Also approach those not currently selling ornaments – these could also be a very good outlet.

Car Boot sales / Market stalls

Nearly every week, winter and summer, there are now local car boot sales and indoor markets where anyone can rent a space or a stall to sell almost anything. Pay a visit to one or two in your area (see the local paper for details) and see the wide range of goods on sale. You can usually book a space or stall in advance for a small fee.

If you are going to a car boot sale make sure that you take a table with you. Indoor markets usually provide tables but check to make sure. Set up your table carefully – remember presentation is very important – and mark the price of each ornament as most people don't like to ask. Always be prepared to barter a little if people wish too – but work out your lowest price and don't go below it.

For these stalls it is probably best to have a range of ornaments on sale – but make sure that you have more than one of each – and keep a note of the most popular items for future reference.

Garden fetes/local bazaars

These are usually organised by local groups to raise money for themselves or for charity but it may be possible to rent a stall to sell items for yourself. Alternatively you may be able to have a stall if you donate a proportion of the proceeds to the organisers. It's worth a try since people are usually more willing to spend money at such events.

Craft fairs

There are now a number of craft fairs held around the country where people sell craft goods at stalls rather like an indoor market, but also demonstrate their particular craft skill at the same time. Why not set up a stall with finished ornaments but take along a few unfinished as well. These could then be painted or varnished as a demonstration. Dates of suitable craft fairs can be found in craft shops, craft magazines or at your local library. You could also try Exchange and Mart under the Art and Crafts section.

Gardening clubs

Find out if there is a Gardening club in your area. If so, contact the secretary and ask whether you could show them some samples of your goods. You could find this a very profitable outlet with many repeat orders.

You can probably think of other potential outlets – use your imagination and you will find that you can sell as many items as you can make!

Setting your prices

Your prices will of course vary according to the size of your finished ornament and also with the type of finish and the time taken to manufacture the item. As a guide let us firstly consider the garden frog. A 25kg bag of cement will make about 20 frogs so you can see that the cost of each finished frog is very low. The paint or varnish finish will only add a few pence to this.

You should now make an estimate of the time taken to make and finish the frog (not including setting and drying time.) I find that it takes about 10 minutes to mix up the cement and pour into the mould. Add to this about 20 minutes for the various painting stages – total time about 30 minutes. In our experience you will find that the frogs sell quickly at around £3.50 each but if you choose you could easily charge around £5 – a mark up of 1000% and equivalent to around £10 per hour.

You could achieve a bigger mark up on larger items. Don't forget that if you manufacture in batches, as I have described, the 'output per hour' increases – so you can see that big profits really are possible.

I suggest that you experiment a little with prices in the early days. You may like to check what other ornaments are being sold locally – you will probably find the prices higher than those you intend to charge. Do not be tempted to price the items too high to start with. It is much better to build a reputation for quality items at a reasonable price.

Customer complaints

If you do get any complaints this is likely to be due to the paint peeling off after some time as we discussed in a previous section. I recommend that you always offer a replacement ornament or refund the money. Retrieve the ornament from the customer since you will be able to scrape off the old finish and apply a fresh coat of paint. If the ornament is in good condition you will then be able to re-sell it.

If you follow the guidance in this manual you could soon have a very profitable part-time business. Once you reach this stage you may wish to expand. In the next section we will consider a variety of ways in which you can expand your business…

SECTION 5
EXPANDING YOUR BUSINESS

6) **Expanding your business**

I recommend that you start with one or two moulds and take a little time to perfect your technique of both making and finishing the ornaments. As you receive more orders your next step is to buy a second or third mould so that you can make several ornaments in batches. Follow this by adding other moulds to your range, first singly and then in batches.

The important thing then is to increase your sales outlets. I still believe that word of mouth is a most effective way to sell the ornaments. Give some further thought to getting people to sell for you on a commission basis. You might find that local clubs and organisations which are looking for fund raising ideas may be prepared to sell for you if you make a contribution to their funds. What could be better than an army of salespeople covering your local area!

Stage 2 is to be a little more imaginative with your ornaments. Why restrict the frogs to garden pools? Here are just a few ideas:

Frogs make ideal doorstops inside the house – or very large paperweights. How about a pair of frog bookends? And what about more creative finishing – I have been asked to make 'designer frogs' to match indoor colour schemes. I have even painted frogs in the strip of different football teams as novelty presents for youngsters (seriously!) Be creative and see what ideas you can come up with.

Stage 3 is to expand into associated areas. Consider the garden gnome range including such novelties as Santa Gnomes. You can buy a range of moulds for making indoor ornaments in a variety of materials from Plaster of Paris to casting in metal. You could specialise in chess sets – time consuming but profitable since you can charge a good price for the finished sets. You could also consider the manufacture of paving slabs and ornamental screening blocks – all made from moulds. And don't forget the moulding of ornamental candles in coloured wax – this alone could be very profitable. Finally you can purchase materials with which you can make your own latex moulds, perhaps from models you have made yourself.

Once you get involved in the business you will find that there really is enormous scope. The sky's the limit! Well, that's just about it but the final section I have summarized the main points of this manual and prepared an action plan for you to follow…

7) **Summary**

In this manual I have described the profitable business of manufacturing and selling garden ornaments. You have seen how to select your product range, how to manufacture and finish your ornaments, where to sell the items and how to expand your business when the time is right.

I have given you as much help as I can – now it's really up to you. I am convinced that if you follow the guidance in this manual you can make money – and have a lot of fun too!

Over the page I have proposed an action plan and I hope you do take action and I wish you the very best of luck…

8) Action plan

- Read the manual once again.
- Contact the mould manufacturers
- Select and purchase your first mould
- Gather together your materials
- Roll up your sleeves and HAVE A GO!
- If your first ornament doesn't turn out that well – please don't just give up, Try again!
- Follow the plan and you can and will succeed!

9) <u>Keep smiling</u>

I know Turn Pence Into Pounds will help you in your quest for your fortune. The information you have learned will stand you in good stead. It will work for you, but only if you apply it! I can give that guarantee because I know it works because it is working for millions of others too.

There will be only one reason why it won't work for you - and that will be because you haven't taken action. Nothing comes easy - least of all success. But you have the information and knowhow before you now! It will never be easier for you to succeed. Refer to this book as often as you need to. Use it as your guide to success - to help you achieve your dream. Before you begin your journey to your future, think carefully about what you want out of life.

Do you just want to be rich? If so, what happens then? There are so many people who started their own business with the intention of getting rich. They wanted the best that life had to offer. But when they achieved it, they weren't happy.

They had gone from using money as a means of achieving the life they wanted, to just amassing money for the sake of it. It never made them happy; they never enjoyed what it could buy them. It was simply a collection of zeros on their bank statement. And they became recluses, Slaves to the process of making more and more money - money which they would never enjoy.

As I have said before, enjoy what you do. Don't let the act of making money become an end in itself. Take time out to actually enjoy your money.

Even if it's only now and again!

Keep smiling, and it will all be worthwhile...

GOOD LUCK!

OTHER TITLES FROM THE PHOENIX RANGE

UP & RUNNING

A BUSINESS OPPORTUNITY MANUAL

WHAT THIS MANUAL WILL GIVE YOU

It is fair to say that absolutely anyone can start their own business. You simply choose a name, inform Inland Revenue and the DSS, and away you go! The problem comes in making it into a profitable enterprise.

Although anyone can start a business, not everyone will be successful, and get rich. I had always thought there must be some big secret to getting rich and successful. And I was right! I spent nine months asking the rich how they made it and I'll spend the rest of my life being glad I did!

Getting rich is NOT the product of good fortune. It is the outcome of putting certain principles and secrets to work for you. Within this manual are the secrets and techniques of the rich and successful.

If you are serious about wanting to make your fortune, and are willing to put in a hell of a lot of hard work, this manual is just what you need. Making the transition from employed to self-employed is not always easy, and useful advice is often hard to get.

Within this book you will find all the information you need. Apply the principles given, and there is no reason why you won't become richer than you could imagine. Success is possible for anyone who really wants it.

YOU REALLY CAN BECOME YOUR OWN BOSS!

Available from PHOENIX PUBLICATIONS
RRP Price £ 29.95

(10% Discount offered to existing customers quoting the barcode on the back of this book)

OTHER TITLES FROM THE PHOENIX RANGE

IMPORT – EXPORT FROM HOME!

A BUSINESS OPPORTUNITY MANUAL

WHAT THIS MANUAL WILL GIVE YOU

As you may or may not be aware, back in 1992 the trade barriers within Europe were lifted and consequently Europe has been well and truly 'OPEN FOR BUSINESS' ever since. Europe offers a vast market to the Import – Export type of business, with people who are just as eager to do business with us as we are with them!

NOW WE CAN HELP YOU TO BREAK INTO THE EUROPEAN MARKET!

No stone is left unturned in 'IMPORT - EXPORT FROM HOME' and subjects covered include the following:

- Setting up your new business.
- What to Import - Export & what NOT to.
- How to Import – Export.
- Overseas contacts & how to get them.

As well as the above, the manual contains much, much more and is a positive mine of information, quite indispensable to the individual who aims to trade overseas.

On a final point, it is worth noting that Import – Export is one of the most lucrative businesses available to virtually anybody who has the desire and drive to set –up such a business. Many, many Import – Export MILLIONAIRES are dotted around the globe – will YOU be joining them?

Available from PHOENIX PUBLICATIONS

RRP Price £ 24.95

(10% Discount offered to existing customers quoting the barcode on the back of this book)

OTHER TITLES FROM THE PHOENIX RANGE

ONE PERCENT OF A MILLION IS £10,000

A BUSINESS OPPORTUNITY MANUAL

WHAT THIS MANUAL WILL GIVE YOU

This manual will introduce you to one of the most exiting and profitable businesses imaginable. It's a business with so many possibilities and variations that just about anyone can start up and make you almost IMMEDIATE MONEY. Whether you're looking for a full time, Highly paid occupation or just some spare time pin money to help pay for the car, you can use this business manual to do it.

The business is SELLING ON COMMISSION. Thousands and thousands of men and women throughout the world have used commission selling as their first step to wealth and success. There is no reason why you shouldn't take the same route!

In this guide we'll be looking at just a few of the many methods of commission selling. You'll learn how you can become a top salesperson while controlling your own business. We'll tell you how you can make your mark in international trade without moving from your home. If you don't like the idea of selling 'face to face', don't worry. You can sell by post and online and still earn up to 50% commission on every sale you make.

However, we'll start with something very simple, very easy to understand and also very easy to do- yet which is still capable of yielding a very substantial income whether done full or part-time

ANYONE CAN DO THIS, EVEN YOU!

Available from PHOENIX PUBLICATIONS

RRP Price £ 24.95

(10% Discount offered to existing customers quoting the barcode on the back of this book)

REMEMBER THIS MANUAL IS YOUR STEP-BY-STEP GUIDE TO A VERY LUCRATIVE HOME BASED BUSINESS.

THE FROG WAY!

www.ingramcontent.com/pod-product-compliance
Ingram Content Group UK Ltd.
Pitfield, Milton Keynes, MK11 3LW, UK
UKHW060050240426
12048UKWH00019B/1417